Life Stories

&

Hilarious Anecdotes

by

Dr Jay

Dedicated to all my beloved friends with whom I have spent numerous hours in various venues, talking about these life stories and laughing about the hilarious anecdotes in this book.

Foreword

All the 'life stories' in this short book are true incidents I have come across, though the names of the characters are fictional. Some of them are from my medical college days in Trivandrum, Kerala, India, where I had studied for M.B.B.S. Looking back about fifty years and writing about the incidents in the medical school was an interesting experience. Some of the events happened when I was in Nigeria from 1975 to 1979, working in a remote village. I left Nigeria in 1979 for higher studies in England. After obtaining the F.R.C.S (Fellowship of the Royal College of Surgeons), and the D.Urol (Diploma in Urology) from the University of London, I worked in the NHS for over thirty-three years and retired in 2013. *Your Lives in Our Hands* is the first book I had published on Amazon, a collection of short stories, all true incidents I had experienced as a trainee in surgery in England.

Some of the 'hilarious anecdotes' are also based on events that had actually happened. For example, 'The Chop', 'The Cooling Period', 'What Shall I Call You?', 'The Freelance Driver', 'The Industrious Student', 'The Loving Boyfriend' etc. are created around past incidents. The stories about 'The Biology Professor' and 'The Forgetful Principal' have been circulating among friends, but considering the characters involved, are entirely plausible.

This book consists of some life stories you may consider quite solemn and serious, therefore I have deliberately added the section of hilarious anecdotes so that any potential reader may have a laugh too.

Life cannot always be too serious, can it?

A Dangerous Encounter

In the third week of October 1968, the mandatory medical check-up and other admission formalities were over and the first year students had begun to attend classes in Trivandrum Medical School in Kerala, India. Ragging, the unavoidable evil every new student had to put up with, was in full swing. The second years, who had undergone the same ordeal the previous year, were looking forward to their privilege to play seniors at the expense of the newcomers. In the name of initiation rituals every sadistic trait they had harboured would come to the fore in their treatment of the immediate juniors. Alas, the principal, though a thoroughly decent gentleman, was adamant that the first year students should wear white coats. Wearing the white coats revealed the identity of the first year batch and they were sitting ducks to be easily targeted by the seniors.

On the second day of medical student life I was already late to get to the anatomy dissection hall, having been stopped and gleefully questioned by a few seniors on my way. Eventually, I reached the junction of two roads in the campus, one of which would lead to the library and the other to the front entrance of the lecture halls from where I could easily make my way to the dissection hall on the first floor.

That was where Fahd Ismail, a second year student, met me and gave me his hilarious instructions.

'Hey, you! Come here.'

I had no choice. The tone of his voice was menacing and he was commanding, not requesting.

'Stand here at this junction and be a traffic policeman. You can direct cars to the library or the front entrance.'

I was to stand there at that junction of these two roads and pretend to be a traffic policeman stopping and directing cars on their way. There I was, clad in all white, white trousers, white shirt and white hospital coat, announcing to the whole world that I was a first year student.

The drivers of the oncoming cars, most of them being doctors themselves, saw the spectacle and chuckled to themselves, while I was getting anxious that I would be late for the first anatomy lesson. After a few minutes I looked around. My nemesis was nowhere to be seen. Fahd had disappeared.

I hurriedly left my new employment as a traffic constable and speedily walked towards the staircase which would take me to the dissection hall.

Lo and behold, Fahd was stood at the foot of the stairs holding up some first year lady students from going up the stairs. He was revelling in his opportunity to talk rudely to some young ladies who were all alone. I pretended that I didn't see him and walked up the stairs past him. He was furious.

'Where do you think you are going? I told you to stand at the junction and direct the oncoming cars.'

I must confess that I had not taken in the severity of ragging in Trivandrum Medical College or the consequences of disobeying an instruction from one of the seniors. It was early days in a protracted season of subjugation and humiliation. The first night in the men's hostel was rather worrying, a taste of what was to come. All of us who had moustaches were ordered to shave them off. Everybody obliged, albeit unhappily. We were all assembled in a room and some general instructions were proclaimed. We were not supposed to ask any of the seniors their names. We had to address them all as 'sir'. A few of them revealed their names voluntarily. One said he was 'God' and that he had to be addressed only as God. The proceedings that night had told me to be reverential to the seniors, but I had not fully grasped the seriousness of the situation. That was why I defended my decision to go upstairs.

'Sir, I am already late for the anatomy dissection class.'

An angry Fahd wanted to show off in front of the female students. He grabbed me by my white coat and a couple of buttons fell on the floor. I felt demeaned and disgraced. It was as if a couple of my front teeth had fallen out. I don't know what possessed me – was it the presence of my lady classmates witnessing my shame? – but I caught hold of both ends of his shirt collar so tightly that it almost choked him. Fahd was not a big man, certainly shorter and smaller than me. Knowing full well that a physical tussle with me in front of the female witnesses was not a good idea, he suddenly let go of my coat while thinking aloud.

'Are you becoming angry? All right, I will sort you out. You wait and see.'

Fahd walked away from us. I went upstairs followed by the ladies. All that afternoon in the anatomy dissection hall I was thinking about what had happened. I told myself that I should not have reacted in that way. He made it clear he would exact revenge and it would be painful for me. I dreaded what would happen in the evening in the men's hostel when other seniors come to know about my dangerous encounter with Fahd Ismail. Maybe Fahd himself would direct proceedings against me. Any of the first year students who dared to resist ragging would be singled out and severely punished, physically and verbally. That was the unwritten rule there.

There were a couple of my cousins in the fourth year batch who had reassured me that they would help if I was in any serious trouble. In the evening I approached one of them and told him what had happened. Unfortunately, I couldn't tell him the name of my adversary as I knew his name to be Fahd, only after the ragging season was over and our moustaches were allowed to grow back to their previous glory. I had a torrid time of physical and emotional abuse during the three months of ragging like all other first year guys, but what saved me from disaster was the fact that Fahd was a day scholar and he didn't come to the men's hostel looking for me.

The Anatomy Practical Exam

The fear of failure hovered around the anatomy dissection hall haunting most candidates like me. An air of anxiety and trepidation pervaded the atmosphere and an unbearable tension was eminently palpable in that hall. Would-be doctors in white coats were waiting, their scalpels sharpened and forceps ready. The acrid, penetrating stench of formalin soaked flesh would have punched a hole in any nostril, yet they were patiently waiting by their respective tables beside the cadavers, or what remained of them, kept ready and prepared for the impending dissections.

Soon the assignment for each candidate in the examination was given out. The embalmed body on the table in front of us was in a prone position. I had to 'demonstrate the structures under the left gluteus maximus muscle'. My friend Harry's task was to 'expose the left kidney'.

I went about what I thought was expected of me, demolishing the skin and fat from the backside to get at the structures beneath the gluteus maximus. To my surprise the skin was as tough as the hide of a pachyderm. Well treated and prepared with formalin and other preservatives during the process of embalming, it was more oily and slippery than was apparent at first sight. The scalpel I had borrowed for that fateful occasion from one of my more studious friends was sharper than I thought it would be, and within a few minutes it escaped my careful attention and attacked my left index finger. Blood seeped out covering the whole finger gradually spreading to the palm of the hand. It was not a pretty sight. One of the tutors in attendance saw what was happening.

She hurriedly managed to fetch a wad of tissues from somewhere which I wrapped around the bleeding finger. I thanked God that I already had immunisation against tetanus.

Thereafter, rather subdued by the accident and resigned to an outcome of failure, I continued my mission of uncovering what was under the gluteus maximus. Soon there was a large pile of skin, fat and muscle in front of me. A reasonably sized molehill! Before I knew it, the time was up and we had to wait for the examiners to come and inspect our dissected material and ask us questions.

Standing next to me was Harry who had dutifully 'exposed' the left kidney. He had cut out a square area and made a window, exhibiting the kidney for any interested passer-by to behold. He didn't realise that he was expected to dissect and show the different layers of tissues in an orderly manner so that the kidney could eventually be seen by the examiners underneath the structures covering it. Instead, he had made a rather large hole in the shape of a window, well and truly exposing the kidney. He was standing there pleased with himself and his performance, confidently awaiting the arrival of the examiners.

Prof 'P' the tough external examiner, breezed in, accompanied by that lovely lady Prof 'S', our professor of anatomy. He approached Harry first and after just one look, he said, 'So, you got an exposure of the kidney?'

'Yes, sir,' Harry answered confidently.

'And you have exposed the kidney, I can see. What is your number?' Prof P asked again.

'Ninety-eight.'

'You can go.'

Harry was a little surprised that he didn't have to answer any questions.

Prof S was disappointed and slightly embarrassed. As a kind and compassionate internal examiner, she felt sorry for her candidate and ventured to ask Prof P if he was not going to ask Harry any questions.

'If you want to ask him some questions you go ahead,' he replied.

A few helpful questions from madam followed and Harry mumbled out some answers, suspecting that everything was not hunky-dory. When the ordeal was over he walked away, a touch puzzled.

The examining team moved towards me. After one look at the molehill in front of me Prof P said, 'Oh! You also are very good at knife work.'

I had kept the injured finger on my left hand well concealed, the whole left arm kept hidden behind me. His comment was made without seeing the finger wrapped in blood-stained tissues.

'What is your number?' he asked.

'Ninety-five,' I said rather gingerly.

'You can also go,' was the remark from the external examiner.

This time madam did not say a word. There were no questions and I walked the glum walk of a defeated man.

Later on when both of us returned to the dissection hall to join the failed additional batch of students for further enlightenment in anatomy before the next exam, our tutor told us cheerfully with a smile as wide as that of a Cheshire cat, 'I knew you would come back. Previously, you were always reading novels and other books hidden in the hard cover of Cunningham (anatomy dissection manual).' We were stunned and speechless. How did she know that?

Sweet Slumber

Some afternoon lecture classes in pathology were so boring that one could easily become sleepy. (Forgive me, I am referring only to the lazy students of the male species.)

We had a decent, unassuming, calm, and cool pathology lecturer. Let us call him 'B'. In spite of his admirable character and conduct, he was too soft spoken. Often his whispering, monotonous speech and his low murmuring voice were not clearly audible to the back benchers in the absence of any contraption even resembling a megaphone in that large lecture hall. No wonder some of us had an inevitable urge to sleep. The fact that we had perhaps had a card game or two the previous night (only till the milk van arrives in the early morning hours. That was the not-so-strict stipulation before any game started) may have been a contributory factor, but sleep we did. Leaning the head on the tall desk and sleeping was feasible, but on the very last benches high up in the gallery, sparsely occupied as they were, lying down and sleeping was also an option which we adopted from time to time. It was not a very comfortable experience, keeping one's head on a hard, wooden bench cushioned on a notebook or a couple of papers brought into the classroom as if we would write notes on them.

One weekend when Harry returned from his home in Cochin, he brought a clever device with him and told me that the problem of uncomfortable sleeping in the class was over. It was an inflatable air pillow! It was very thin, like two papers put together, but a comfortable pillow when blown up with air. At first, I was surprised at the audacity of this young guy (he was but a teenager of nineteen), but later on decided to join in the adventure with him. I told him, 'Buddy, you will have to share the luxury if you want any secrecy about this.'

He readily agreed. Thereafter we used to sleep lying down with our heads resting comfortably on an inflated pillow. Accurate timing was the key. In a huge lecture hall with 185 students, when the attendance roll call was over Dr B would turn to clear the blackboard or perhaps write something on it. One of us would suddenly disappear at that moment, lying flat on the bench behind the tall desk and start inflating the pillow. Of course, we took turns making the pillow available to one of us on alternate pathology lectures. To be fair to Harry, the owner, I used it less than he did.

One day in the pathology practical class, students were excited about something called a 'giant cell'. Everyone wanted to see it. The demonstrators and tutors were in demand. The assistant professors overseeing the conduct of the practical classes were also in attendance, helping inquisitive students. I decided to call for help from Dr B who was roaming around, his arms held in a clasp behind his back. My clever idea was to simply show my eagerness to learn and thereby enter his good books.

Dr B duly arrived and I asked him if he would kindly show me what a giant cell looked like as I couldn't find it among the numerous cells seen on the slide. He slowly bent his head down, looked at the slide under the microscope, made some adjustments to the apparatus to obtain an accurate focus, and without raising his head, asked me, 'You are Harry and your friend standing over there is John?'

I swiftly corrected him.

'No, sir. He is Harry and I am John.'

I was quite pleased that he was willingly engaging me in a conversation.

Dr B continued without averting his gaze from the slide under the microscope.

'Okay. Why are you interested in pathology practical classes? In theory classes both of you are sleeping, sometimes sitting down, sometimes lying down. Why this great interest in the giant cell now?'

I stood there as if I were thunderstruck. I was astounded and dumbfounded all at once. It was like a total eclipse but somehow, I didn't faint. Suddenly, at a stroke, it dawned on me that he was watching our shenanigans all the time in the lecture hall but was kind enough not to banish us from his classes or call us up and punish us. He had thought better of it and was decent enough to let it be.

I wished that I could vanish into thin air. I stood there looking at the floor, guilty and ashamed, the attempted scoring of a brownie point having boomeranged and turned out to be an own goal. Dr B slowly raised his head from the microscope and said, 'If you have a look now, what you see in the centre of the slide is a giant cell.'

Without another word he walked away gracefully leaving me totally deflated.

An Awesome Challenge

It was the beginning of December. The Harmattan dust storm from the Western Sahara desert was already wreaking havoc, sweeping across Nigeria. There was dust everywhere. Any surface, be it table, chair or sofa had to be wiped with wet cloths. An unavoidable seasonal nuisance.

In the evening when we were about to have our dinner I had a call from the hospital. 'A call' doesn't mean a telephone call. Oh no! There was no such luxury. It simply means that one of the nurses walked over to my residence in the hospital quarters for doctors clutching a notebook with the details of a patient I was supposed to see. The manner of her walking, or her running, usually gave away the seriousness of the situation. The 'doctors' quarters' was a semi-detached house about 500 metres from the main building of the hospital where there were inpatient wards, outpatient clinic rooms and an operation theatre.

This, I noticed, was in fact a leisurely walk. That usually meant that the patient was conscious and talking.

In the emergency admissions unit I saw Maria, a young Nigerian woman who looked like a sheet of white paper. She was brought in the back of an old, dilapidated, spluttering hatchback, a Toyota Corolla. There were no visible external injuries. She told me that she was all right till she suddenly felt faint and fell down. No, she didn't hit her head anywhere.

There were no diagnostic tools like ultrasound or CT scan in 1977. In those days we depended on careful history taking and our clinical examination. When I asked her about her monthly periods Maria said she had not had any for about ten weeks. She was a married woman and was trying to have a baby. I asked her, 'Has your tummy become bigger since you fainted?'

'Yes.'

'Any discomfort in your shoulder?'

'Yes,' she admitted.

Examining her I confirmed that she was severely anaemic and that there was free fluid in her abdomen. I reached my firm diagnosis. This twenty- year old has had a ruptured ectopic pregnancy and her abdomen is swollen with a lot of blood in it. She had a rodeo ride along the bush roads, traversing the bumps and potholes and losing blood with every up and down exercise.

Just to complicate the situation a touch, I was told that they belonged to the 'Jehovah's Witness sect and that they didn't want Maria to have a blood transfusion for fear of excommunication from their church. The relatives and elders who came with her were adamant.

I had a choice, an unenviable choice: I could refuse to treat her in our hospital, citing lack of facilities and send her to a different Christian mission hospital thirty miles away in the back of the said Toyota Corolla for another rodeo ride, or I could take the huge risk of a death on the table and operate on her there and then in our theatre without wasting time. If I send her away, she will almost certainly die on her way to the other hospital. In any case, I swiftly started her on an intravenous infusion of a crystalloid solution, attempting to bring her blood pressure a bit higher. Then I called her husband aside away from the others. He was begging me to save her. I told him, 'I will try my best if you would allow me to transfuse her with her own blood in the theatre during the operation.

13

Your relatives wouldn't know about this because it would just be a part of the procedure I am going to do.'

He readily agreed so I decided to take on the ultimate challenge.

I had only read about 'auto transfusion' in surgical text books. 'Necessity is the mother of invention' they say. (Don't they also say 'desperate situations call for desperate measures'?) I decided to go ahead and do the auto transfusion which I had never seen done in my young surgical life.

There was a significant problem. In that remote village hospital, we didn't have the luxury of an anaesthetist. The only two doctors there were my wife and I and my wife was a junior doctor who had just completed her house officer posts. All the operations I had done in that hospital were under local anaesthetic infiltration of the incision site, aided by some sedation.

Electricity was available when the generator was switched on for a couple of hours in the mornings, a few hours in the evening and whenever I had to do an operation in the theatre. The generator was already on because this emergency was during the evening hours.

Let me cut the story short. I prayed to God fervently and begged for the life of this young woman, scooped the blood out of her abdomen (peritoneal cavity), filtered it and got it into the transfusion bottles with the help of the nurses and my wife assisting me. It was fresh, uncontaminated blood of the patient herself. There was no need for cross matching. Thus, Maria was given two units of her own blood and the operation to remove her ruptured left fallopian tube was done as fast as I could. Thank God, Maria had a smooth post-operative recovery and she was discharged from the hospital after eight days.

Later on, after four years of service under most challenging circumstances, I left that village hospital for higher surgical training in England. The nun sisters gave me and my wife a grand send off. In the audience there was an extremely grateful Maria with tearful eyes who had come to say thank you to us. I was rather emotional too, when I made a 'vote of thanks' speech in front of the large crowd assembled there. My wife was rather embarrassed.

'You should have been stronger. Why did you have to weep like a child standing on that stage in front of a multitude?'

Certainly, an exaggeration! A wife is a wife. I didn't answer her.

Unexpected Visitors

I was told that there were a couple of people waiting outside the labour room to see me. The Nigerian nurse who brought me the message also said, 'They look like your friends or relatives. Your wife is also with them.'

At first I was bewildered. It was only 10 am on a Monday morning, a working day. An unannounced visit from friends or relatives at that time was unlikely. It was quite baffling to me. My wife Lucy, the only other doctor in that hospital, was supposed to be doing a very busy clinic at that time. I became anxious and concerned.

The diagnosis of twins had been made simply by the palpation of two heads in that pregnant woman's uterus. There was no facility for ultrasound scanning in that Catholic mission hospital in a remote village in the East Central State of Nigeria in 1976. Even in Western countries regular ultrasound scanning for pregnant women became routinely available only in later years.

The first baby, a healthy baby boy, was already out and I was patiently waiting for the next one to make an appearance down the exit pathway. That was when the message about some unexpected visitors was delivered to me. Usually, soon after the first baby is born, the twin will also follow without too much delay. I waited patiently, all the time wondering why those people were waiting outside the labour room to see me. The second baby, however, was not in any hurry to make its appearance. Twin babies are, normally, smaller in size. That is why the arrival of the second one shouldn't take that long. The senior nurse in the labour room who was checking the

16

woman in labour and monitoring her progress announced, 'Maybe the delay is because it is a breech presentation.'

Eventually a baby girl made her way down. I left the labour room only after making sure that the placenta was also delivered, there was no excessive bleeding and the babies and their mother were safe and well.

The two young men waiting to see me were new faces, people I had never seen before. My wife had red eyes suggesting that she had been crying earlier. She looked sad and upset as if she had heard some terrible news. Still, she managed to tell me, 'They are from Enugu. They are cousins of Raju who was with us yesterday afternoon.'

She stopped and looked at the guys.

One of them said, 'I am Sunny, Raju's first cousin. This is Joseph. He is my friend who offered to accompany me because he is familiar with the roads around here. Actually, he knows this area well.'

I nodded, shook their hands and said, 'Yes?' prompting him to go on and explain what this unexpected visit was all about.

'After Raju, Dolly and your other friends left your place yesterday afternoon, the car in which they travelled was involved in an accident.'

'Oh no!'

Maybe I was afraid of enquiring what had happened. Instead, I simply asked, 'Where was this?'

'Just a few miles before reaching Aba. An oncoming truck hit the car. A head-on collision. The Nigerian driver Augustine, Mr Kurian, and his ten year old son Soman died instantly. Dolly was taken to the Catholic mission hospital in Aba. The senior doctor there, Dr Thampi, tried his level best but he couldn't save her. Raju was the only survivor. He escaped with fractured legs and some broken ribs.'

Sunny continued.

'Dr Thampi telephoned me from Aba early in the morning when he got my number from Raju. We are on our way to Aba. I was told that Raju was your classmate. We wondered if you would like to come with us. The bodies will be buried in a church cemetery in Port Harcourt this evening.'

I looked at my wife Lucy. She was crying.

Raju was a student at Catholicate College Pathenamthitta, in Kerala, at the same time as me. He was studying for a biology degree when I was reading chemistry. For the language classes, English and Malayalam, we were together in the same hall. After graduation I entered the medical college and he went on to read for the M.Sc degree in biology. It was by chance that we had met in a supermarket in Aba where he was employed as a teacher in a secondary school. I invited him and his wife Dolly to come and visit us in our residence in the hospital quarters in the village of Etiti near Umuahia.

Ever since our meeting in the supermarket, Raju and his wife used to visit us from time to time. Dolly loved spending time with our daughter Anne who was two years old. Dolly had a little girl of the same age whom she had left back home in Kerala with her parents, because she was worried that the child would get malaria which was rampant in Nigeria. Spending time with our Anne was a blissful experience for Dolly, as if she were spending time with her own daughter of the same age left in India.

The previous afternoon we had visitors. Mr Thomas Kurian, an accountant working in a reputable firm in Port Harcourt and his ten year-old son Soman, had gone to

Ihyala to see a relative. His wife was ill with a nasty chest infection and had decided not to accompany her husband and son. Kurian travelled in his white Volvo car driven by his driver Augustine. On their way he had picked up Raju and Dolly from Aba, offering them a lift to Owerri where they spent the weekend with friends. On their return journey all of them stopped by our hospital to see us. We had a lovely time together and after coffee and light refreshments we asked them, 'Why don't you join us for dinner?'

They declined saying, 'As you know, it is not wise or safe to travel at night in this part of the world.'

After the Biafran war there were too many guns at large and some of the old soldiers, now unemployed, would turn highway robbers at night to get some easy money. Dolly spent quite some time with our daughter, cuddling and kissing her and saying that the child had an unbelievable resemblance to her own child left in India.

The news of the tragic accident was a terrible shock. I said to my wife, 'Why don't you take these gentlemen to our residence and give them something to drink? They may be tired after the long trip from Enugu. I will talk to the matron in charge and come and join you.'

Lucy nodded in agreement.

The matron, Sister Mary Anne, was very empathetic and compassionate when she heard about the tragedy. She instructed the nurses to explain to the patients what had happened and to cancel the outpatient clinics.

I rushed back to our residence, a semi-detached house in the hospital campus provided by the authorities free of charge. The other half of the house was empty because the second doctor in the hospital, for whom it was meant, was my wife Lucy. Being fully furnished, it was occasionally used by the Bishop of Umuahia who had responsibility for overseeing the administration of the hospital.

I considered the situation and told my wife, 'You don't have to travel with me to Aba. It is better that you stay here with Anne. It is not appropriate to take her to Aba at this time.'

Lucy agreed. Sunny and Joseph travelled in their car and I went ahead of them in my car as I was more familiar with the route to the hospital where my friend Dr Thampi was looking after Raju.

Driving the car on the road from Umuahia to Aba, one was reminded of the perils of travelling on that particular road or any other road between two major towns in Nigeria. Cars, lorries and trucks on the opposite side, were whistling past my car on that narrow road. It was not a dual carriageway. Buses were almost non-existent and most people travelled by car. Of course, there were lorries transporting goods and people from one town to another. I recall that one of my close friends who had not yet bought a car after arriving in Ibadan had to travel almost 250 miles on the back of a lorry to come and visit me in Umuahia.

On my way to Aba I could identify the spot where the horrific accident had happened the previous evening. I recognised the crushed and crumbled metal remains of what was the white Volvo car in which my friends had travelled. Along the way one could see that the road to Aba was littered with several such wrecked remnants of various vehicles of different makes, shapes and sizes as a result of the accidents that had occurred in the previous weeks and months. Prompt removal of these metal carcasses was not a priority item in the 'to do' list of the authorities.

I managed to dodge and weave my car through the chaos of the traffic jam in Aba town centre. The visitors from Enugu following my car close behind must have struggled to keep up with me. Eventually we arrived at 'Sacred Heart' Catholic Mission Hospital in Aba town centre and were relieved to find that there were parking spaces for more than two cars in front of the hospital.

Dr Thampi had cancelled his clinics and other activities scheduled for the day. He delegated all his responsibilities to his colleague, a Nigerian doctor working as his assistant. We went into the private single room where Raju was sleeping under heavy sedation, his legs in plaster casts elevated in stirrups that hung from above. After a few minutes he opened his eyes and saw us. He wept uncontrollably, tears streaming down his cheeks. He didn't utter a word to us.

Thampi had told him that Dolly was too ill and was being looked after in the intensive care unit. He must have feared the worst and seen through the falsehood of that statement that was deliberately meant to keep him calm but misinformed. He didn't ask any questions and just stared blankly ahead. After a while Raju went back to sleep.

Outside the room Thampi told us, 'Kurian's Malayali friends, with the permission of his distraught wife, have decided that the bodies would be buried at Port Harcourt this evening. Would you like to attend the funeral?'

Kurian had his grieving widow woefully mourning the loss of her husband and son at a stroke. Dolly had nobody in Port Harcourt or in any other part of Nigeria. Raju was confined to a hospital bed in Aba unable to move, let alone travel to attend his beloved wife's funeral. I decided that I certainly would attend the funeral service and bid farewell to Dolly on behalf of her husband. It was getting late so if I was to get to the church service on time I would have to move. Thampi offered to take me to Port Harcourt in his car because he was more familiar with the town and the roads than me. We entrusted Sunny to break the bad news to his cousin when we were on our way. The nursing sister was asked to keep Raju sedated with the painkillers already prescribed.

There was a huge crowd of Indians and Nigerians to attend the funeral ceremony at the church. We got there just in time to attend the service. I told myself, 'There is nobody among this crowd here who had known the person inside the fourth coffin except me. I am the only one who had known the twentysix year -old Dolly, at least for a short period in her young life.'

The Nigerian priest made a brief but poignant speech, warning all those assembled there about the fragility of human lives. He reminded the congregation that nobody had a permanent residence on planet earth and that all of us had to move on, whatever the circumstance of our demise. He urged everyone to seek God's grace, to be nourished by their faith, to help one another and do what was favourable in God's sight while we had our life in this world. I was very sad when I left Port Harcourt. Thampi was trying to make conversation but I kept my participation minimal. All I could say was, 'Thampi, thank you for coming with me, and thank you for all your valiant efforts to save Dolly. You know, I am so pleased that we could attend the service. Otherwise, a young wife and mother, the daughter of two loving parents back home in Kerala, would have been buried without anyone in that large crowd representing her husband or her relatives.'

After a few months when he was well enough to leave the hospital Raju came to visit us. By nature, he was a quiet, unassuming and humble man, but after his appalling loss he was also a broken man. Raju had resigned his job and was to leave Nigeria in a few weeks. He thanked me for attending the church service on behalf of him. He also said, 'On the evening when the accident happened, back home in Kerala our two- year old daughter was crying incessantly without any apparent cause. Being the early morning hours in Kerala, she was sleeping but she suddenly woke up and started crying inconsolably. The baffled grandparents tried their level best to calm her down but apparently the child cried all night!'

Wishful Thinking!

The telephone rang. Not the mobile. The genuine one, the one with the Sky Shield. The voice from Sky asked my permission to allow a call from Glasgow. I agreed. There was an excited sounding woman on the line. She said, 'Can I speak to Mr Thomas please?'

'Mr Thomas speaking.'

In a cute Glaswegian accent, the lady asked me 'For security reasons, could you please tell me the first line of your address?'

'159 Burton Road,' I replied.

'And the postcode please.'

I was getting irritated but I complied with her request,

'BN21 2DU.'

'Congratulations, Mr Thomas, you have won the jackpot in this month's draw of the premium bond numbers.'

She was almost shouting over the phone, I thought.

I couldn't believe it. Is someone trying to trick me into a scam?

It can't be an April fool call because the month is February.

The voice from Glasgow could palpate my disbelief but she continued.

'Don't be sceptical. This is true. You have only £250 in the NS&I account. You have the option of buying more bonds till the maximum of 50,000 bonds is reached. The remainder of the prize money can be paid into your bank account. Where would you like us to deposit the money? Can we use your joint account details we already have on our records?'

I still couldn't believe it but I had to say something. It is unlikely to be a con job because she is not asking for bank details, only asking permission to deposit the amount into the account details they already have.

'Okay,' I said. I then asked her, 'Is it safe to deposit a huge amount into a current account?'

'The banks have strong security built in, but it may be wise for you to move the money into deposit accounts, preferably in multiple banks, as soon as you receive the amount,' she advised.

Did I feel a bit dizzy? I was holding on to the shelf on which the home telephone was placed, lest I should fall down. The Glaswegian lady decided to leave me alone to chew the matter over. She once again confirmed that £49,750 will be invested in further purchase of premium bonds and the remainder of the one million pounds will be placed in the joint account of Mr and Mrs Thomas in the Eastbourne branch of HSBC. After saying congratulations once more she ended the call.

I slowly walked to the living room and collapsed on the sofa. My wife asked who was on the phone.

Disguising any incredulity or jubilation, I asked her to come downstairs.

I may have conveyed a sense of urgency as she came down the steps in a hurry.

'What's the matter?'

I smiled a broad smile and said, 'I have won the jackpot in the premium bond draw this month.'

'What? No way. It is somebody trying to con you into giving them more money. Don't fall for it. You are too naïve as always.'

Her advice was serious with a sting in its tail.

Then I calmly explained to her the whole conversation I had with the cute voice from Glasgow.

'We have nothing to lose anyway. I will go to the bank this evening. An electronic transfer may not take long. These transactions are done instantly these days you know.'

When the news and the credibility of it gradually sank in, she decided to take credit for the

blessing from above.

'I was the one who bought the premium bonds for £250. It was a present to you on our twenty-fifth wedding anniversary,' she tried to convince me.

It was not true. It was the other way round. She wouldn't dream of buying glorified lottery tickets worth that amount, even though the capital was safe in the case of premium bonds. I didn't contest her claim, chuckling to myself instead. Maybe she was just pulling my leg. My mood on that occasion was one of subdued elation, not indignant confrontation.

She ran upstairs to ring our daughters and tell them the good news, with a caution that all this maybe a hoax, just fool's gold.

Downstairs I was carefully dividing up the amount. 'Okay, £200,000, that is one fifth, will be set apart for good causes.' Various charities would benefit, especially the ones dear to my heart: Eastbourne Food Bank, Mathew 25, Christians Against Poverty, Salvation Army, Smile

Train, Barnardo's, Water Aid. I had a long list of my favourites.

The remainder of the mortgage will be paid off and some money will be kept for old age nursing home care for the two of us. The remainder will be divided equally between our two daughters.

Will my wife agree? I know, I am naïve.

Only a Monkey Nut, a Surprise Nonetheless

The Christmas break was fabulous. It was an internal holiday, not a trip abroad, a get-together with the family in Brighton. Mathew travelled by train which was overcrowded but there was no hassle of check-ins, no long queues for security checks, no tedium of baggage collections, not even the congested traffic on the M1, M25 and M23 to deal with. A train journey for the family gathering for Christmas. It was great. When the bubble eventually burst it was disappointment when you realised that you have to wait another year for a repeat of the marvellous occasion.

Back to the real world in January 2020. The schools had reopened. After a couple of weeks away Mathew went back home, again by train. Using the key carefully kept in his trouser pocket he opened the door of his house, collected the mail off the floor, mainly Christmas cards and advertisement leaflets, and went to the kitchen.

He was surprised to see a monkey nut on the kitchen floor. He clearly remembered hoovering and wiping that floor before he had left the house. Where had this come from?

On his way to the stairs he noticed that the door to the dining room was slightly open. He usually keeps it closed. It was quite windy the previous day. Maybe that had something to do with it. He walked upstairs and found that the curtains were drawn. Lo and behold, the dressing table drawers were half open. All of them! Then it dawned on him. Someone had entered that two-bedroomed detached house in his absence.

He went downstairs again and found the back window of the dining room was open. The lock on the handle was intact but the window was open. Hells bells! Has anything been taken? He darted to the kitchen table where the spare key to the Lexus GS 300 had been casually left in the oval-shaped fruit tray. Thank God, it was still there. The car must still be in the garage. Quickly, he went into the study room. There were two laptops there, one three- year old HP and one twelve-year old Dell. Both were untouched. Thank God, again.

The situation had soon evolved into a crisis management scenario when Mathew called the police emergency number and was then advised to call the non-emergency number. He tried that new number and was told that the forensic team would ring him back.

After a while a lady police officer came in her 'police scientific technical support' vehicle. She was very pleasant, very supportive and very experienced. After her investigations using some black powder and brushes and different coloured wipes, she pronounced, 'They prised open the back window using a screwdriver and scrambled in, head-first, through the top half of the window. They had worn gloves leaving no fingerprints. They were looking for cash or jewellery. They were not interested in laptops or cars.'

Mathew told the officer, 'They must have been hungry but I had left nothing in the fridge. The only edible stuff was a packet of monkey nuts in the bottom cupboard. That's gone apart from the single one on the floor.'

Travelling by Pod

The date of our trans-Atlantic journey from Heathrow Airport was fast approaching. There was excitement as well as a tinge of trepidation and my wife and I were wondering how to get there from Eastbourne. A taxi would be too expensive, even a dedicated airport taxi from Polegate. Of course, I could drive to the airport on the day and park the car in the long stay car park for ten days. That was a reasonable option but the possibility of being stuck on the motorways, M23 or M25, and the plane taking off without us was a worrying one. It doesn't normally happen but it could. Our tickets were not refundable and hence the enhanced anxiety. We eventually decided to adopt the safer option of travelling to the airport the previous day and staying in a hotel nearby.

Trawling the various relevant web-sites, we stumbled on an excellent deal. Staying the night at the Thistle hotel near Terminal 5 and parking the car in their car park for ten days, with transportation to the airport by pod thrown in as well, all included in a reasonably priced package. We were delighted.

On the previous evening of our journey, religiously following the instructions of the lady on the Satnav, I managed to get to the Thistle hotel in the vicinity of Terminal 5 and park our car in the car park in front of it. At reception they didn't ask for the key of the car, just the registration number. That was a relief. The young man at the desk told us that when we were ready to go to the airport the following morning, we should go through the double doors opposite the reception desk and follow the green lines painted on the pavement till we got to Station B in the car park at the rear of the hotel. He gave us a four-digit PIN and continued, 'the green lines will take you to a steel gate. By the side of the gate there is a small machine on which you have to enter the given PIN number to open the gate. Thereafter, if you follow the green lines you will reach Station B where you will see the pod. It will take you to Terminal 5.'

Another four-digit code was provided which we had to type on the keyboard of the machine in Station B so that we could get in the pod. We were advised to keep both PIN numbers safe as we would need them for the return journey.

For any of you who is wondering what a pod is, let me explain that it is a driverless electric vehicle which would take you from the car park to the airport terminal and the same in reverse on your return journey.

Like little children we were excited about the travel by pod, something we had never experienced before. Our overnight stay in the hotel was comfortable. Coffee, even the decaffeinated variety, and tea, even the green variety, and caramel biscuits were provided free in the room. The next day arrived. A beautiful day with not a cloud in sight, no April showers, just glorious sunshine! Rolling our luggage on wheels along the green lines, we arrived in front of the huge steel gate and entered the magic PIN number in the machine in front of us. Nothing happened.

'Move away, let me try,' my wife said (she always tries to score one over me).

She tried once and then again. No success. Thankfully, we could contact reception via a speakerphone to ask for help. They managed to open the gate by remote control and I forcibly pushed it open. We happily rolled our luggage on till we arrived at Station B.

There it was! The pod! It looked as if it were a capsule detached from the London Eye. Interestingly, apart from us there was nobody there at Station B, no queue or crowd of passengers struggling to get into the vehicle. There were no railway staff and not even any security officials for safety checks. In fact, Station B was just an area in the rear car park of the Thistle hotel. We entered the appropriate PIN number on the small machine in front of us and lo and behold the doors of the pod opened. It was a comfortable six-seater carriage, grey and black in colour. The moment we got in a lady's voice in a posh accent said, 'If you are comfortably seated and your luggage safely secured, please press the start button for Heathrow Airport.'

My wife eagerly pressed the button next to the sign that said 'Start' and off we went. Five miles of wonderful driverless journey followed. On its predestined track the pod went straight at first, then up a slope and then down the slope and straight again. It felt like being on a ride at Thorpe Park. The pod took us along the flyover and we saw the endless rows of cars beneath us on the motorway in both directions. On our way we also saw another pod on the adjacent track going in the opposite direction, carrying passengers back to Station B, to the Thistle hotel's rear car park. When we got to car park 2 of Terminal 5 there was the voice of the posh lady again: 'You have reached your destination, Terminal 5, car park 2. Airport departures are from car park 5. Bye, bye.' The doors opened automatically.

On our way back the pod was dutifully waiting for us at car park 2. Travelling back to the hotel I wondered aloud, 'What if this contraption breaks down? What will we do? They may have to lift the whole capsule in a helicopter or something.'

'Don't be silly,' my wife reprimanded me.

Angel Delight

It was a beautiful sunny July afternoon in the lovely scenic village of Alfriston in East Sussex. Amy, a twenty-one year old university student, asked her mother, 'Mum, can we go to Southampton and sort out some stuff in my flat? It is a lovely day today.'

'Yeah, that's a good idea. After all, we can only do these things when you're on holiday. When the new term starts you won't have time for anything. It's my day off so I can come with you,' her mother Lilly replied.

'If we go immediately after lunch, we'll have time to tidy up the place and buy some essentials from the supermarket. It doesn't get dark until after 8.30pm. We'll be able to come back tonight.'

'All right then. Let's have an early lunch and then leave. I want to get back as soon as possible.'

Listening to their daughter moaning daily about her university accommodation and observing the pathetic state of their communal kitchen, Amy's parents eventually decided to buy her a flat in Southampton. Amy managed to rent out one of the two bedrooms in the flat to a fellow student and dear friend, but it was her responsibility to keep the place tidy, furnished and well equipped.

Having failed to inherit her mother's gene for punctuality, Amy was chastised: 'Come on, Amy! Why are you always "last minute.com" whenever we need to go somewhere? It's always the same. Get a move on or we won't be able to come back today!'

Soon after lunch mother and daughter were on their way in Amy's new maroon Nissan Micra. As was her usual practice, Amy, a committed Christian, said a quick prayer before she started the engine. Later in the week she had to do some preparations for leading a service on Sunday at the local Baptist church. The topic that the minister had chosen for the sermon that week seemed unusual to her. The subject of 'angels' was not one she had heard previously, despite attending church services for many years. Oh well, she'd just have to decide how to introduce the topic later in the week. For now, to improve her mother's mood, she decided to play her favourite CD, 'ABBA Gold', in the car.

Just after they had passed Worthing, true to the unpredictability of the British weather, the atmosphere changed. It turned cloudy and dark. After a short time they were on the dual carriageway approaching Littlehampton. There was a downpour of heavy rain and all the cars slowed down. Thankfully, it was a short burst and soon it was only a light drizzle so Amy turned down the windscreen wipers to a low speed.

On the slow left lane of the dual carriageway there was a huge lorry, slowly creeping its way uphill. Lilly was rather impatient. She asked her daughter, 'Why don't you overtake this one? We'll be behind it all day at this rate.'

Amy signalled to move to the lane to her right. She was still cautious on the roads, having passed her driving test only a few months previously. She dutifully checked her wing mirror and blind spot to ensure that no car was approaching from behind and mused that her driving instructor would have been proud. Impressing her mum, who was still rather annoyed by her lack of punctuality, was undoubtedly a secondary motive. When she was certain that it was safe, Amy moved to the right lane and attempted to overtake the lorry. As the Nissan Micra came parallel to the lorry and the car reached about 50mph, Amy suddenly realised in horror that the car had taken on a mind of its own. The vehicle lunged to one side, abruptly skidding and spinning around 360 degrees. Amy tried desperately to control the car but the steering wheel simply did not respond to her commands. The front of the car hit the back of the lorry and it spun as it rebounded. Terror and panic struck both women. In the chaos, Amy cried out, 'Mum, what shall I do?'

Lilly yelled back, 'Just hold on to the steering wheel!'

The car spun yet again and swerved from the road towards the metal barrier between the two dual carriageways. Certain that the car would topple over into the oncoming traffic, Amy's life flashed before her eyes. She was staring death in the face and so her thoughts turned to the loved ones she would never see again. What was the last thing I said to my sister? she wondered. Did I say a proper goodbye to Dad?

Amy applied the brake with all her might, almost standing on the pedal. After what seemed like an eternity, she finally regained control of the car and the Micra stopped in its tracks. Fortunately, there was no car behind them in the fast lane. There were several cars on the left and their drivers watched the spectacle anxiously as they drove past.

The lorry had pulled over and a couple of cars behind it did the same with their hazard lights flashing. The driver of the lorry came out and inspected his vehicle. When he was satisfied there was no damage done, he promptly drove off without stopping to see what had happened to the small car or its occupants.

The atmosphere inside the car was unbearable and Agnetha's hauntingly beautiful voice from the CD was suddenly grossly out of place. Amy's first thought was for her mother – was she alive? She turned off the music and shot a look at her. 'Mum, are you okay?' The look of stunned horror and disbelief on her face told Amy that her mother was alive and, thank God, uninjured. Her next thought was to the cars behind her. She was gripped with a paralysing fear. Was anyone behind her injured... or worse? Amy was speechless, frozen to her seat, her white-knuckled fingers still gripping the steering wheel following the nightmare of what had just occurred.

Most of the small cars which had stopped on the dual carriageway drove away, just like the driver of the lorry. All except one. A young lady of about twenty years of age clad in pure white trousers and white T-shirt sporting a silver star approached the Micra which, like its owner, was still fixed in place. Amy was startled to see the young woman knocking at the driver's window. The young lady gently opened the driver's door and asked, 'Are you all right?'

The terrified mother and daughter nodded in agreement without saying a word. The woman introduced herself. 'I'm Angela. I saw what happened, I was a few cars behind you. Thank God both of you are all right.'

She walked around the Micra to assess the damage to the car. She came back to the driver's side and looked at Amy. 'What's your name?'

Amy replied but even the sound of her own voice was muffled, strange and unreal, as though she was speaking from beyond the grave.

'Well, Amy, the car is only slightly damaged on the front of the bonnet and the wing above the right front wheel.' She smiled reassuringly and added, 'You can let go of the steering wheel now.'

Having regained at least part of her composure, Amy asked, 'What happened to the drivers behind? Is everyone okay?'

'Yes, Amy. No one was injured and even the lorry got away without a scratch. Now, I need you to step outside the vehicle and look at the front of the car with me. It's damaged but not beyond repair.' Observing the terror on Amy's face, she added, 'I'm right here. When you stand up your legs will feel like jelly and you'll think you're about to collapse. You won't. I'm here and I'll be holding you.' Amy was on autopilot. There was something about Angela that was enormously comforting. She was in control and could be trusted. Amy stood up. Right away her knees gave way from under her, but sure enough Angela was right there, in front of her, holding both hands firmly. She led her around the car. Amy held back the tears when she saw the front of her beloved first car, smashed up and broken.

'Now, Amy,' continued Angela in a calm and almost nonchalant manner, 'just reverse your car back and follow my car into the nearest lay-by which is about 200 yards away. The car's still in working order. There's no great damage,' she smiled.

'No. I'm not driving ever again. Mum, can you do it?'

But Angela looked directly at Amy and spoke with confidence. 'No, your mum can't do this, it has to be you, Amy. It's like falling off a horse. You just have to get straight back on again.'

'But I can't... I just can't,' Amy pleaded.

Angela smiled. Again she spoke with a cool, encouraging voice.

'Amy, can I ask what you do for a living?'

Surprised, Amy replied, 'I'm a medical student.'

Angela responded, 'Well then, you know you have to drive this car. When you're a qualified doctor you will need a driving license. I can guarantee that if you don't do it now you will never have the confidence to drive. You can do this. I'll be right in front of you, it's only a few yards.'

There it was again, that comforting reassurance, the aura of genuine concern and protection. Pointing ahead she continued, 'Park your car in the lay-by next to mine. You have no time to lose. There will be a police car here any minute. Before that we need to drive into the lay-by.'

Amy reluctantly decided to do what was suggested. Surprisingly, the car started easily as if nothing had happened. She reversed the car and followed Angela's small silver vehicle into the lay-by where there were enough parking spaces for five cars. Amy noticed a van already parked there with a vendor selling refreshments from it. Before she knew it Angela had opened the front door of the Micra on the passenger side. She said, 'Well done! Now, I'm going to get a coffee for you both. You're still in shock so it'll be sugary!'

Before she could say, 'No, thanks,' Angela was already buying the drinks at the van.

Shortly afterwards, just as Angela had predicted, a police car went past blaring its siren. 'Don't worry,' Angela observed, 'they'll drive past a few times but they won't see us.' Amy wondered how Angela could speak with such certainty. After all, the police were bound to be looking for a car that had been involved in an accident, and here was the Micra with its front bonnet smashed in!

Sure enough, after a few minutes the police vehicle was seen again, sounding its alarm and showing off its blue revolving lights. Amy felt the panic rising within her again but her fears were unfounded. Angela's words proved prophetic. The police car never spotted the Micra and it didn't reappear a third time. Glancing over at the troubled young driver, Angela kindly remarked, 'You didn't do anything wrong, Amy. The road surfaces are treacherous around here, especially in damp conditions. The car skidded and it could have happened to anyone.' The words were like a healing balm and Amy was profoundly grateful.

The next few minutes were a blur to Amy and her mother as they sat down next to Angela near the van, watching cars shoot past them on the A27. Shortly afterwards, and much to their amazement, an RAC vehicle arrived. Amy and Lilly looked enquiringly at Angela who had taken the liberty of calling the RAC to certify the Micra roadworthy. Astonished by her foresight and kindness, Amy asked how Angela knew that her breakdown cover was with the RAC. She smiled knowingly. 'Why, there's a sticker on your windscreen!'

After the RAC chap had given the 'all clear' and left, Angela stood up. 'Well, I must be off now, Amy. When you drive back home be confident. Nobody is going to notice the car. Here's my mobile number and my address. If you need any help whatsoever please let me know.'

It was Lilly who replied.

'Angela, we don't know how to thank you. I am not sure what we would have done without your help.'

'Don't worry. Please contact me if you need anything. Bye.'

Angela hugged both Amy and Lilly before driving away. Mother and daughter looked at each other and then at Angela's silvery white Ford Fiesta fading into the distance.

A sense of sadness descended upon Amy at the departure of this incredible young woman. She looked at the piece of paper containing Angela's address. She smiled at the thought of this amazing young woman living in a place called 'Mount Pleasant'. How very apt. Amy got into the car and she prayed again. Her Christian faith had always been important to her and she was desperate to get home without any further problems. It was her firm belief that the outcome of the journey would have been far worse had she not benefitted from God's protection during the crash and afterwards. She gingerly got back onto the dual carriageway and eventually arrived back at Alfriston.

The irony of the topic for the Sunday's sermon did not fail to escape Amy. She told her mother, 'Mum, I may have had my doubts before, but I really think Angela was our guardian angel today! You believe in them, don't you?'

Lilly replied, 'Dressed in white with a permanent smile and a compassionate look, she certainly looked like an angel. Isn't it striking that her name was "Angela"? Read in Malayalam, the language spoken in Kerala where I am from. It would mean "I am an angel".'

Pentharaphobia (fear of the mother-in-law)

Mary was tossing and turning in her bed in the middle of the night. She found it somewhat better when she was lying on the left side. The size of the full-term uterus leaning against the liver was the reason for the discomfort when she was on her right side. (Being a medical graduate herself she was familiar with human anatomy.) The 'due date' was only a couple days away and the baby inside was kicking her rather hard from time to time. 'It must be a boy this time,' she decided, judging by the ferocity of the kicks. She couldn't go back to sleep after lying awake for about half an hour. She recalled the famous lines written by a Malayali poet who, in one of his poems, eulogised how comfortably any pregnant lady would carry the baby in her womb, even if wearing a flower may seem too heavy for her at that time.

How untrue, she thought.

'What does he know?'

Of course, the poet was only trying to pay a tribute to all women going through the ordeal of pregnancy. Alas! Belonging to the male species, he was blissfully unaware of the scale of the discomfort of a fully pregnant woman. She remembered what her husband Raju told her the previous day. Apparently, according to the famous Welsh poet W.H Davies, there were three things more beautiful than any man could wish to see, the third of which was a young woman showing her baby before it was born.

Mary told herself grudgingly, 'Watching from the side lines, these guys can dish out all the romantic sweeteners they like, but they don't have to toss and turn in their beds in the middle of the night worrying about what is to come.'

Mary was genuinely apprehensive. During her first pregnancy her mother was with her, always watching over her like a guardian angel. Of course, it was six years ago in 1975, in Kerala, South India. She'd had the best care available; the Professor of Obstetrics, who had taught her in the medical school, was in the labour room herself, overseeing the delivery of the baby and yelling out instructions to the midwife and the junior doctor in attendance. Raju was away in Zambia where he had gone to take up his first job overseas, just three months previously. Mary knew that even if he was around, he would not have been allowed in the labour room to be by her side. The traditions and customs in Kerala at the time would not have permitted him to go into the labour room to be with his wife, even if he wanted to. The delivery and arrival of her sweet little baby, Manju, was a prolonged and extremely painful affair. (Mary had always resented the fact that Raju was not there to witness her agony!) The position of the baby in the womb was 'occipito-posterior', a difficult presentation of babies during labour. The experienced professor who was quick to scold and shout at her assistant junior doctor and the midwife was nevertheless kind to Mary and very attentive of her.

In Preston the consultant obstetrician in charge was not going to turn up and deliver this baby. In fact, when Mary was admitted to the hospital with a miscarriage the previous year even the registrar did not attend her, in spite of the fact that Mary was a young doctor herself even though she had not started working in England. In the early morning hours, it was the senior house officer (SHO) in obstetrics who carried out the procedure of dilatation and curettage (D&C), to remove the retained products of conception from the uterus.

When Mary was desperately trying to catch up with some sleep, turning to her right and then her left, Raju was working as the 'on call' duty doctor that night for emergency surgical admissions in Preston District General Hospital. He was always very busy with major responsibilities in general surgery. His studying and preparing for the Primary Examination of the Fellowship of the Royal College of Surgeons (F.R.C.S) didn't help either. For Raju, it was like climbing Everest, being totally unfamiliar with the multiple-choice format of that tough examination of basic sciences (with minus marks for the wrong answers). Back in Kerala, for his M.B.B.S examinations there were only essays and short notes to write. Those from the sub-continent who had done the deed (passed the primary examination) behaved as if they were a cut above the poor sods who had not.

The new SHO in surgery, Dr Kishore Kumar, was a typical example. Unlike his colleagues he walked with a swagger because he had just passed the F.R.C.S primary. It was generally accepted that the final part of the F.R.C.S, being a clinical examination, was easier than the primary which mercilessly scrutinised the candidate's grasp of the basic sciences. No wonder those who had passed the primary acted like they had already obtained the coveted accolade, the four magic letters of F.R.C.S widely perceived as the license to wield a knife in the operation theatre.

Dr Kumar, also from India, hailed from Lukhnow in Utter Pradesh. He and his wife Bindu lived in a house on Winchester Road just opposite where Raju and Mary lived. It was one of the houses set apart by the hospital as accommodation for doctors with families. Bindu was not a doctor. A tall, lean woman of fair complexion, she was very friendly with Mary and her six- year old daughter Manju. Dr Kumar was a couple of inches shorter than her but she always made an effort to avoid standing next to him. In his presence she was very quiet and subdued.

Within a short period Bindu was a frequent visitor to Mary's house and the two women were always talking about their respective families back home. The conversations had to be in English because Mary had not lived in North India and therefore couldn't speak Hindi; her mother tongue was Malayalam which was the language spoken in Kerala. Soon it became clear to her that Bindu was in fact Dr Kumar's first cousin, the daughter of his father's older sister. Mary was surprised. She told her friend, 'In Kerala among some Hindu families there is a system called "Mura Pennu" which means "destined bride", a practice whereby girls were predestined to be married to their first cousins. It is a long held tradition which ensured that the family property or assets would not have to be parted with when a girl was being given away in marriage. Any dowry or share of possessions given to her will remain in the same family. That arrangement was slowly dying out. I was not aware that it happened in North India as well.'

Bindu replied, 'Oh! It is a common custom where I come from.'

She frequently spoke to Mary about her mother-in-law being jealous and resentful of her, even though the woman was her father's own sister. She said she was afraid of her because she was too intrusive and bossy.

Lying in bed and thinking about the impending delivery, Mary wondered what would happen if the baby arrived when Raju was on call. She knew that his leave would start in a couple of days. Who will look after Manju when Raju would be with her in hospital at the time of the delivery? There was Dr Malhotra with his family living in one of the houses nearby, who might be happy to keep her in their home for a short period. But they had two children of their own to look after. Mary decided that Bindu would be the most appropriate person to help because her house was just a few yards away on the opposite side of the road, and being newly married she didn't have any children yet. Her thoughts were interrupted by a pang of sharp pain across her lower abdomen. Simultaneously she felt wet down below and realised that her water had broken. She recognised the inevitable and bleeped her husband.

'It looks like the baby is on the way. Get here as soon as possible.'

Raju got one of his colleagues to cover him for the rest of the night. By the time he arrived, the contractions were increasing in frequency and Mary was getting more and more anxious. Soon they had to be on their way to the hospital. Manju, the six-year old, was asleep. Raju woke her up and walked across to Dr Kumar's house with her. On the way he told the child, 'You are going to sleep in Bindu aunty's house tonight. I have to take Mummy to hospital now. You have to be a good girl. Okay?'

The sleepy child agreed, perhaps not knowing what she had agreed to.

Raju knocked on the door. It was Kishore Kumar who opened it. When he heard that Mary had to be taken to hospital he said, 'We'll look after the little one, mate. Don't worry about her. You'd better get back to your wife. Hope everything goes well.'

Raju was relieved. He left Manju with Bindu who had come downstairs by then and rushed back because the ambulance had already arrived to collect Mary.

The birth of their baby boy was uneventful. In spite of the unavoidable huffing and puffing and pushing and shoving, the whole ordeal was quicker and less painful for

Mary than the previous time. She was pleased that Raju was in the labour room, holding her hands and kissing her on her forehead from time to time. There was no need for even an episiotomy this time.

'It's a boy, Mary!' Raju sounded ecstatic, albeit a little too loud. Before Mary could see the baby, who had slowly emerged out of her after her last push, her husband had noticed the tiny 'willy' and he happily proclaimed the sex of the baby. It was as if he had won the lottery. Mary was just relieved that the whole saga was over and that the baby was crying as normal healthy new born babies do.

The next day after collecting Manju from the Kumar household, Raju took her to see her baby brother. On the way the little girl told him that Bindu aunty had looked after her very well.

'I had cornflakes, a boiled egg and milk for breakfast. Bindu aunty was very nice. Daddy, I can go and sleep there again if you want.'

'No, baby. The hospital has allowed Daddy to have leave from today onwards. You don't have to go to their house tonight.'

Manju was delighted to see her baby brother. She thought that the baby was too tiny but cute. She said she would call him 'Arun'. She had selected that name some time ago with the tacit approval of her mother, assuming that it was going to be a baby boy.

After a couple of days when Bindu came to see the baby, she reported to Mary that Manju was a lovely girl who had behaved impeccably when she was with them.

'You can leave her with me any day. She won't be a problem for me.'

The days after the birth of the new baby went more smoothly than Mary had envisaged, and the little girl, Manju, was as good as gold. In addition to what Mary had cooked and kept in the fridge and the freezer, Raju managed to make some rice and a curry according to his wife's instructions and guidance. He was pleased with himself about that accomplishment because he had never done it before. In his very busy job, he hardly had any time to help his wife in the kitchen. (Mary was secretly pleased that he wouldn't make her kitchen messy.)

A few weeks later, Dr Kumar paid them a visit. Mary thought it rather odd that Bindu had not accompanied her husband. She recalled that in fact Bindu had not come to see her for several days. After the customary chit-chat Kumar dropped a bombshell, as it were. He told Raju and Mary, 'I came to tell you that we've lost Bindu's diamond necklace.'

The shock of the news was still fresh in their minds when Kumar went on to say, 'The only person who had been in our house recently was Manju whom we had looked after at the time when Mary was in hospital.'

Kumar said that he had already informed the police about his loss. When the officers asked him about any recent visitors to the house, he told them that Manju was the only outsider to have entered their house recently. Mary and Raju were astounded that this man had already told police about the little girl sleeping in that house for a few hours! Kumar continued the story. 'The police had wanted to speak to the child even if she was only six years old. I didn't agree to that. The officers were adamant. They said they couldn't carry out any investigation if they were not allowed to interview the child. So, I told them not to proceed any further. I came here today to ask the little girl if she had seen the necklace or taken it and kept it out of curiosity.'

Flabbergasted at this explosive revelation, Raju was speechless for a few seconds. When he regained his composure, he told his colleague, 'Kishore, you should have asked the police to continue the investigation. That way any doubts you or Bindu had would have been cleared up. In any case, you can talk to Manju now. Here she is.'

The little girl was already standing there clinging to her mother's sari and listening to the conversation between the adults. She was scared stiff, worried that she would be taken before the police, but she didn't cry. Her baby brother, Arun, started wailing abruptly for no apparent reason. Up to that time he had been lying quietly and happily in his mother's arms, looking at her as if he was carefully studying the features of her face. Did he, by some extra sensory perception, smell the fear and anxiety which had gripped his sister? Or was it just a bit of trapped wind in his tummy? Suspecting the latter, his mother held him upright and patted him on his back a few times; he kept quiet after a while.

Manju plucked up the courage to tell Kishore uncle, 'Uncle, I didn't see any necklace. I just went to sleep after Bindu aunty tucked me in bed. In the morning she gave me breakfast and she did not show me any necklace.'

Asking the parents not to have any ill feeling towards him because of these developments, Kishore Kumar quietly left. Mary was sad that he didn't reassure them that he believed the child or that he didn't suspect her anymore. The whole saga had shaken Mary and Raju to the core. They were sorry to hear that the diamond necklace was lost but furious and incredulous that their innocent child considered a suspect.

'Thank God for small mercies. He came here to tell us that he had been gracious enough to prevent the police from interviewing our child. A great favour!' Raju said sarcastically.

Soon after this incident the Kumar family went to India for two weeks to visit their parents. When they came back Bindu paid Mary a visit. She had brought some sweets, halva and jilebi, for Manju and announced proudly that they were home-made. After a brief description of their trip and the viciousness of the hot weather in Lucknow, she implored Mary, 'Mary, please can you keep a secret if I tell you something? Don't tell anybody, even your husband, okay?'

Mary agreed.

'The diamond necklace was never lost,' she said.

Mary couldn't believe her ears.

Bindu said that she had kept it hidden in the house and told Kumar a lie because she didn't want to take the necklace with her to India.

She did not want her mother-in-law to get her hands on the precious necklace which her parents had given her as a wedding gift. She was genuinely afraid of the woman and her frequent interferences in her married life. It was a true case of pentheraphobia, the fear of the mother-in-law.

All the aggravation, the report to the police and the unjustified suspicion of an innocent little girl were because of Bindu's fear of her mother-in-law! Bindu had wilfully created a smokescreen to hide behind and keep hold of her precious possession, the diamond necklace. She came to tell her friend the truth because she couldn't live with a guilty conscience any longer. Mary promised her that she would keep it a secret, but when Raju came home that evening, she promptly told him everything. Both of them were indignant that their daughter, an innocent child of six, had a shadow of suspicion cast over her in the eyes of one man whose wife had fed him a lie. Sworn to secrecy, Mary didn't want any further strife from the affair and she successfully persuaded

Raju not to confront Kishore Kumar with the information from his wife.

Having completed two years in the same job in general surgery, it was time for Raju to move on. He had applied for a job in Epsom as an SHO in orthopaedics and got it.

A few days before the family left Preston and went to Epsom, Bindu came to say goodbye to Mary. She had brought with her a beautiful new dress for Manju.

Stung by remorse, she must have considered it a reasonable gift to alleviate some of the anguish she had caused the little girl and her parents.

Manju was delighted. When Bindu was gone, she said, 'What a beautiful dress, Mummy! That Bindu aunty is such a nice lady, isn't she?'

Mary paused for a second and then replied, 'Yes, dear.'

Headlong into Christmas

Christmas had arrived and as always excitement was in the air, though not rooted in the jubilation for the birth of Jesus Christ, the saviour of the world. Oh no, it is all about shopping. Headlong shopping for the celebration of a festival, shopping for an apoplexy of indulgence, eating, drinking and 'feeling good' for a prolonged period.

Five years ago, about two weeks before Christmas, my wife and I went to the local Sainsbury's for groceries. We would be lucky to get a parking space and we were watching one family loading up the boot of their car from a huge trolley that was full of stuff. I patiently waited for them to reverse their car and soon they were on their way. I saw that the driver of another car was eyeing the vacated slot but I was ahead of him. I quickly squeezed my car into the empty parking space and breathed a sigh of relief.

Having grabbed a medium sized trolley, I slowly moved towards the entrance of the supermarket. The automatic swing doors opened inviting me in and I pushed the trolley in front of me and was about to walk in.

All of a sudden, the sliding doors closed again trapping me between them. I let go of the trolley and tried to wriggle out of there with some urgency, my instinct for self-preservation having kicked in. Alas, my head was stuck tight between the doors but my body was somehow able to squirm, twist and break free. Lucy, my wife, and the other onlookers were aghast. The security man at the door shouted something to someone. After about a minute the doors opened again. My two ears had borne the brunt of the ordeal. They must have looked bright red and in a sorry state.

'Are you all right?' Lucy asked me. The same question was repeated by several others who rushed to the scene.

When I recovered my composure I answered, 'I think so.' I gently ran my fingers over my ears and made sure that there was no bleeding. Having worked as a registrar in one of the busiest Accident and Emergency departments in England for a whole year, I knew a thing or two about minor and major injuries so I was pretty certain that I had not come to any serious harm. Many onlookers suggested that I should get myself seen in the A&E department at the DGH. They pointed out that it would be a useful record for any future legal action against the store. I thanked them all and said that I would be fine.

The store was teeming with people and there was a huge Christmas tree with 'Christmassy' frills, trappings and trimmings. The background music over the loudspeaker in the store was based on carol songs or their adaptations. The Sainsbury's employees were all wearing some Christmas decoration on their persons, be it a curved, red woollen cap or a smiling miniature Santa pinned on their clothes.

Soon I found out what had happened. The department store was trying to do one of their mandatory fire drills. Without warning the customers and preventing their entry to the store by posting employees outside the entrance, someone just closed the doors. I happened to be the unfortunate guy who got trapped. The security man who was a witness to this saga told me that everything was recorded on CCTV cameras installed in the store. Some of the friendly onlookers said that I should definitely sue Sainsbury's for a potentially fatal accident. I smiled and thanked them and replied that I would think about it.

One of the lady employees at the store came running and introduced herself to me as the assistant store manager. She asked me to tell her what happened so that my version of the story could be recorded in a safety incident book in the store. After finishing her writing she assured me that she would inform the authorities about what had happened. I made it clear that I would expect to be contacted by Sainsbury's and emphasised that a similar negligence in care should never ever happen to another customer in the future.

On our way back home Lucy, who was furious, reminded me about the advice from well-wishers about suing the store. I was pleased and relieved that I was safe and that I didn't sustain any serious injury. I reminded her, 'There is some hapless man or woman in charge of that fire drill who would probably be punished by the big shots in the superstore hierarchy if I took matters too far. I would never want that to happen.'

A few weeks later I got a letter from Sainsbury's apologising for the trauma and inconvenience I had experienced in one of their stores. Enclosed with the letter were coupons worth £70 inviting me for another headlong shopping trip to Sainsbury's! 'Be thankful for small mercies' they say, don't they?

Where has James Gone?

It was in the middle of my walk in the morning. In the spring when there was no rain forecast it was better to get the walk done in the morning and get that all important exercise over with. After all, that was the only time you were allowed outdoors if you were a seventy-something old man strictly advised to be confined to your dwelling. Covid-19 had temporarily taken over your life and put paid to any other prospect of adventure in the outside world.

I was approaching the halfway mark of my fifty-minute trek along the well paved walkways in Lower Willingdon. In the peak of the lockdown there were hardly any cars on the roads, just a few people walking their dogs and a few others, just like me, taking a walk. If you spotted them first you would swiftly move across to the other side of the road. Social distancing, you see, one of the most important weapons in your armoury for the fight against the invisible but deadly foe. Just as I was walking past the Co-operative store by the side of Linfield Road, I saw a human figure, rather tall, lean and unkempt, clad in worn out shabby clothes. He was standing beside the entrance to the car park in front of the store.

Keeping a safe distance, I walked on when I heard, 'Excuse me. Could you spare two pounds?'

I was stopped in my tracks. He didn't have a mask on, nor did I. In those days the expert advice was not strongly in favour of masks, especially when walking outdoors. I was wearing my jeans, my walking attire which didn't have my wallet in it. Alas, I didn't have a penny on me. Making sure that I was not too close, I told him the truth. I don't think he believed me. He had a resigned look with the facial expression declaring, 'I've heard it all, mate.'

I felt sorry for the man as he may have been hungry. Standing in front of the entrance to a food store he was, perhaps, trying to buy a loaf of bread and some milk with the two pounds he had requested. I know, I was being naïve you would say. He could have been a drug addict who burnt his dole money and other state benefits on drinks and drugs. He could have been an unsavoury character who would have posed some danger to anybody silly enough to interact with him. Still, I just couldn't walk away from a hungry man asking for two pounds, whatever his past history. I asked him, 'Your name?'

'James.'

'James, I came out for a walk. I don't have any money with me but if you wait here I shall go home, have a shower and come back in my car and give you the money.'

He was sceptical when he asked, 'How long will it take? Can I walk with you to your house?'

Something warned me that James walking with me to my house was not a good idea. I said, 'James, it will take about half an hour only. I will have a quick shower and come back in my car. I promise.'

Albeit unconvinced, the man agreed and I walked as fast as I could.

At home my wife noticed that I was getting into the car to go somewhere immediately after taking a quicker than normal shower. She enquired, 'Where are you going?'

Concerned that she may not approve of my philanthropic adventure if she heard the whole story, I said, 'I shall be back in a few minutes.'

It was already thirty-five minutes since I had walked away from James as I swiftly drove towards the store where I hoped he would be waiting.

Another five minutes and I was in front of the car park entrance. To give him a pleasant surprise and to make up for his wait there I had a twenty- pound note in my pocket, ten times what he had asked for. He would be able to buy bread and milk for a few days at least.

There was no sign of James. He probably didn't believe me and didn't want to wait there in vain. Maybe he waited for half an hour and then left. I felt sad and somewhat guilty. Perhaps I should have told him forty-five minutes rather than thirty minutes when he asked me how long he had to wait.

When I described the incident to my dear wife, she was not very pleased that at the time of the Covid-19 pandemic I had an unnecessary encounter with a stranger, neither of us wearing a mask. She also wondered why I didn't have two pounds on me when I went walking.

Thereafter, every day I walked I had that twenty-pound note in my pocket, but I never saw James again.

Hilarious Anecdotes

The Chop

Out of nowhere a police constable appeared in front of the car beckoning the driver to stop. Emmanuel Kelechukwu, the Principal of Igbobi College, Lagos, Nigeria, stopped his Mercedes abruptly. Allen Smith, an Englishman teaching physics in his department in the same institution, was sitting in the front passenger seat. The policeman entered the car through the rear door. Seated comfortably, he demanded, 'Drive on.' He had wrongly assumed that the white man was the owner of the Mercedes and the black man his driver. Facing Smith, he said, 'Your driver went through the red traffic lights. You have to pay a penalty otherwise I will take you to the police station.'

He anticipated that the 'Oybo' (foreigner) wouldn't fancy a trip to the police station and therefore would give him some money. Smith looked at his colleague.

Kelechukwu protested, 'I did not drive through any red signal! Let's go to the police station.'

Again, the policeman addressed Smith, the white man. This time he was more candid. 'Oga, (Sir/Chief) I am a small man. I chop you small. If we go to the police station the big man there will chop you big. You'd better settle this here and now.'

Kelechukwu replied instantly, 'The big man there was my student at Igbobi College. I am taking you to him.'

The policeman, who had hoped to make a fast buck, realised his folly. Recognising that his ploy had boomeranged he kept quiet. After a few seconds he implored, 'Oga, please stop the car. Let me go.'

Kept for Viewing

Mr Philip Pappadopulous was a resident in Nightingale Nursing Home. He'd had severe memory loss for the last couple of years and of late had become rather unpredictable. He was not violent or aggressive, but his judgement was impaired and he couldn't distinguish between what was proper or improper. It was in keeping with the symptoms of worsening Alzheimer's disease. When he was in his lucid intervals, he was a fairly humorous character. The trouble was, at times, nobody could be sure if he was being humorous or just barmy.

One day the nurses saw him sitting in the living room with his limp penis fully exposed in the presence of other residents, male and female. When Cathy, the named nurse with the responsibility to look after him, saw the spectacle she was aghast. She asked Philip to stop being silly and cover himself up. Pointing to the exposed lifeless organ, he told her, 'He is dead.'

The embarrassed nurse persuaded him to dress properly and he obliged. The next day, in full view of the audience in the living room, Philip again left the zip of his trousers open exposing his penis in full view of others. Again, Cathy saw the scene and she was quick to reproach him asking, 'Philip! What are you doing?'

'He is dead, you see. Now he is lying in state. I have kept him for viewing.'

The Posting in Dermatology

It was in the fourth year of his course at the medical school that Rajmohan had his clinical posting in dermatology. The subjects covered were skin diseases and venereal diseases. Rajmohan was notorious in the men's hostel for his regular drinking sessions, his occasional drug taking and his reckless womanising. He was a well-known absentee from clinical postings in various disciplines. When he decided to attend his posting in dermatology, his friends declared among themselves that Rajmohan was keen to keep up with the signs and symptoms of venereal diseases. It was believed that he was out there attending the clinic for the latest information about the prevention and treatment of sexually transmitted diseases.

In the outpatient clinics patients with different conditions were brought, with their full consent, for the medical students to examine them and learn about various diseases.

On that fateful day a young woman, a sex worker of some ill repute with a sexually transmitted genital ulceration caused by Haemophilus ducreyi, was brought for case discussion. She came into the cubicle where there were five medical students, all clad in their white coats waiting to see her and examine her. It was the Professor of Dermatology, Dr Vidyadharan himself, who brought her in. She had a look at all the would-be doctors and she instantly recognised Rajmohan, one of her frequent customers! In a genuinely surprised voice she exclaimed aloud in Malayalam, *'Anna! Annan medical daacta?'* (Brother! are you a medical doctor?) According to his classmates, Rajmohan jumped through the window and escaped. He was very lucky that the clinic was in a cubicle on the ground floor.

The Cooling Period

It was the biochemistry practical examination for the first-year medical students. Sebastian, well known as a joker among his friends, was standing idly in the laboratory beside a beaker half full of some colourful solution he had made. A tall man with noticeably large eyes bordering on proptosis, he was just standing there looking around in his typical carefree mode, gallantly observing his classmates who were frantically doing experiments in their quest to do well in the examination.

Dr Subhashini, an associate professor in biochemistry, was doing the invigilation, walking about the lab closely monitoring what was going on. Her job was to make sure that the students were not cheating or misbehaving. She noticed Sebastian just standing there without doing anything in particular. She approached him and asked, 'What are you doing? Are you not doing the experiment assigned to you?'

'Oh! No, madam. I am just waiting.'

'Waiting for what?'

'For the solution in the beaker to cool. It is just the cooling period.'

'Cooling period? How do you cool a solution?'

'I just wait till it cools down.'

'Is that how you cool a solution, just by standing lazily beside it?'

'Yes, madam.'

Dr Subhashini was getting irritated but she decided to keep calm. She asked him, 'Suppose somebody gives you a hot cup of coffee just before you are about to go to

college for the morning lecture. How will you cool it?'
(She was expecting an answer like 'I will place the cup in
a bowl of cold water to cool it' or 'I will transfer the
coffee several times to and from another cup to cool it.')

'I will not go to college that morning, madam,'
Sebastian replied, as cool as cucumber.

The ill Relative

Timothy, a 'happily married' man was continually nagged by his wife, Jane. Even when there was no obvious shortcoming from his part, she would always find some complaint to exasperate him with and demand some action from him.

One day Jane said to Tim, 'My cousin Andy has been discharged from hospital. You didn't visit him in the hospital, did you? Why don't you go and see him in his flat at least? He lives all alone. Poor Andy! You have no sympathy in your bones, have you?'

'He was in the mental hospital, wasn't he?'

'Yes, but he is cured now, isn't he? Otherwise, they wouldn't allow him home, would they? C'mon, Tim. Move your butt and go and see him.'

'All right then. Calm down now! I'll go and see him.'

Timothy had bad vibes about this undertaking, but he craved for some peace and tranquillity in his home. He decided that keeping his wife quiet, at least for a while, was worth the effort.

Andy was surprised to see his cousin-in-law, Tim, in his flat. He was very pleased. He said that the treatment in the hospital was very effective.

'I have been cured. My doctor told me that I am all right now. My only problem now is that I have a lot of saliva in my mouth. What about you, Tim? Do you have a lot of saliva in your mouth?'

'No, Andy. I don't.'

'Oh, that is great then! Tim, could you please open your mouth wide? Let me transfer some saliva into your mouth then... Please...'

Tim was disgusted and frightened in equal measure. He had deliberately positioned himself near the front door not knowing how his cousin-in-law would behave. He darted out of the room closing the door behind him and ran as fast as he could, down the stairs and fled towards his car. On the way he shouted, 'Go and spit in your mother's mouth, you crazy idiot.'

The Freelance Driver

Dr Francis Xavier went on holiday to Kerala, India, to visit his relatives. He had retired from the National Health Service (NHS) in England after thirty years of meritorious service as a consultant ophthalmologist.

When he was in Kerala one of his brothers lent him a car and arranged a freelance driver to take him around. Sukumaran, the driver, was popularly known as 'Suku'. He was the driver of their family car several years ago and Francis was pleased to see him again.

Suku said he was delighted to be of help to 'the doctor from England'.

During their first journey to the town Francis told the driver, 'Suku, you are driving too close to the edge of canal.'

'No, doctor, you feel like that because you are sitting in the passenger seat in the back. You are not the first one to tell me this.'

Francis kept quiet but was unconvinced with the explanation. He had genuine concerns about this chap's field of vision. When they reached the town and the car was stationary, he asked the driver, 'Suku, can you close your right eye with your right hand over it and read the letters on the board in front of that shop?'

Suku closed his right eye with his hand held over it and asked, 'What letters? Where? Which shop?'

The man had complete loss of vision in his left eye. Francis advised him not to drive any car anymore and asked him to go and see an eye doctor as soon as possible. Suku agreed. On the way back Francis drove the car himself.

After a couple of days Suku came with the sad news that he was diagnosed to have glaucoma. The eye specialist told him that he was completely blind in his left eye and that his right eye also had partial loss of vision. Suku was strictly advised not to drive anymore. Francis felt sorry for the unfortunate man who had lost his livelihood and gave him some money out of sympathy for his predicament.

On his return journey back to England, Francis had a different driver to take him to the airport. The car stopped at traffic lights. There was a huge lorry loaded with bricks coming from the opposite direction which had also stopped at the traffic lights. To his utter amazement and horror, Francis saw that the driver of that big lorry was none other than Suku, the freelance driver!

The Camouflaged Answer

The Professor of Surgery, Dr Zachariah, was well known for the numerous text books he had written. His books on how to learn anatomy as well as how to do surgery were equally popular with medical students. He took his role as a teacher and mentor for the students under his care very seriously. Education of the next generation of doctors was something he had considered a mission in his life. No wonder he was immensely popular among his junior doctors. Surgical trainees were keen to have a posting in his unit because they knew that he would give them opportunities to do operations under his watchful eyes.

It was Dr Zachariah's practice to visit all the patients on his operation list in the evening prior to the day of the operation. (Most conscientious surgeons all over the world would do these 'ward rounds' to familiarise themselves with the patients, some doing their rounds on the day of the operation.) His aim was to discuss the cases with the surgical trainees for their teaching, explain the procedures to patients, and also to leave any instructions to the nursing staff about the patients posted for the next day.

One day, during his pre-operative ward rounds, one of the patients scheduled for a cholecystectomy (removal of the gall bladder) asked him, 'Doctor, will you be doing my operation?'

Dr Zachariah was known to be an honest man who wouldn't tell a lie. He answered, 'No. It will be Dr Krisna Murthy here who will do the operation. Don't' worry, Mrs Chinnamma, so far Dr Murthy has never had a complication doing this type of operation.'

Obviously, the woman was pleased. What Dr Zachariah didn't tell her was that Dr Murthy had never done this type of operation before!

The Biology Professor

The official medium of instruction was English in the university college in Kerala. Alas! The professor of biology was notorious for his 'broken English'. He was nevertheless adamant that he would speak to his students and staff only in English. No wonder the college campus was awash with stories about his poor standard of the language. In spite of that, he was keen to show that he would strictly adhere to his principle of using the official medium of instruction in verbal as well as written communications.

There were only twenty students in the final year doing a combined degree course of Botany and Zoology. Twelve of them were male students and the remaining eight, female. When Mary Thomas was absent on Friday, the professor asked the other students where she was. He was told that she had left a message for him in the office of the biology department that she was unwell and that she would be back on Monday.

During the weekend the professor learned from reliable sources that his student had gone on a pleasure trip with her family to Thekkady, a famous hill station and wildlife preservation centre, and that was why she was absent on Friday. He was furious that one of his students had fed him a lie.

On Monday morning he called Mary Thomas to his office for a dressing down. Without any effort to hide his anger he asked her, 'Where were you on Friday?'

'I was unwell.'

To make it crystal clear that he knew the truth, he yelled at her, 'That's a lie. You went to Thekkady with your family. Didn't you?'

The young lady was astonished. How did he find out? She kept quiet realising that she had been caught out. The furious professor went on in his not very clever English, 'If you lie with me today, you will lie with the principal tomorrow. Isn't it true?'

Mary Thomas bit her lips and looked down on the floor, trying desperately not to laugh.

Evening Walk

The College Day Celebration held annually in Trivandrum Medical College, in Kerala, was held in an open-air theatre in the beautifully maintained garden in front of the main building of the college. It was a very popular event attended by a large number of students and staff. The principal would make a short speech, declare the function open and hand over the stage to one of the staff who would be the master of ceremony, introducing the various items on the agenda. For the young ladies it was a welcome opportunity to dress up, display their saris, and get out of the women's hostel to attend a function held in the open-air venue. Even for the most studious bookworms of the student community, male or female, it was a function not to be missed.

A small number of young men would have had a drop or two of some liquid of the intoxicating kind prior to their arrival at the auspicious occasion. Their enjoyment of the evening would be buoyed by the additional fluid intake they'd had. They would take care to avoid the front half of the seating arrangement to escape the attention of the staff. Generally, they would be pleased with seats in the back rows where they could talk to each other and pass hilarious comments among themselves for their entertainment.

On one of these grand evenings the proceedings on the stage were progressing with aplomb. A third year student occupying a seat in the last row, Murlidharan, suddenly turned to the left side of the ground and addressed someone in a loud voice, 'Where are you going this cold evening without even a scarf around your neck?'

More than half of the audience who heard him looked to their left to see who was doing the evening walk.

Lo and behold, he was addressing a stray dog!

The Godmother

Carole considered it a privilege to be the godmother of her niece, Celina. She took seriously the promise she had made at the baptism ceremony that she would help bring up the baby in the Christian faith. Time went by and one day Carole went to see Celina who was already four years old. The child was delighted to see her aunty who often brought her presents and told her stories. She was a bubbly little girl, very talkative and happy whenever she had visitors in the house. Being an only child she was often bored without anybody to play with.

That day Carole decided to tell her niece the biblical story of 'The Good Samaritan'. She was keen to instil some Christian compassion in her ward in accordance with her responsibility as godmother.

After describing how robbers had attacked and beaten up a man and left him on the road to die, Carole wanted to talk about the priest who passed by ignoring the seriously ill man. Instead of saying 'priest', a word her niece may not understand, she decided to say 'bishop' and asked Celina, 'Do you know who a bishop is, Celina?'

The answer was immediate.

'Yes. There is a bishop on grandpa's chess board.' (Her grandpa was making audacious attempts to teach her how to play chess! He hated telling stories.)

Carole smiled. After explaining who a bishop was, she went on to say that a judge also passed by the ill man. She asked Celina if she knew who a judge was.

Celina paused, thought about the word 'judge' and said, 'Yes. I know who a judge is. A judge is a man sitting in a chair in *Strictly Come Dancing*.'

Carole gave up.

The Forgetful Principal

It was the inauguration of the cancer centre in the medical college hospital. The principal, Dr Ramakrishnan, was the chairman of the public meeting. Dr P.V. Varughese, the Vice Chancellor of the University of Kerala, was invited to do the inauguration ceremony. Being the chairman, Dr Ramakrishnan was expected to do the introduction speech in the beginning and the conclusion speech at the end.

When all the audience in the auditorium were seated and settled down, Dr Ramakrishnan stood up and did the introduction. The absent minded principal made a huge mistake. He said that he had great pleasure in welcoming Dr Samuel Jacob, the Vice Chancellor of Kerala University, who had kindly accepted his invitation to come and inaugurate the cancer centre. (Knowing fully well that Samuel Jacob was the former chancellor of the university, the baffled audience considered it a slip of the tongue and ignored his gaffe.) He went on for a few minutes welcoming the other guests and sat down. Next, the consultant oncologist, the director of the cancer centre, made a speech about what facilities will be available in the new institution for patients. Dr Ramakrishnan was a bit sleepy at the beginning of that speech and by the time Dr Varughese, the vice chancellor and chief guest, stood up to do the inauguration the blundering principal had fallen asleep!

Dr Varughese started his speech saying, 'I am afraid I have to correct your principal. I am not Dr Samuel Jacob. He was the previous vice chancellor. I am Dr P.V. Varughese.'

The audience who had already noticed with alarm the error the principal had made laughed heartily. Dr

Ramakrishnan was in sweet slumber, unaware of all this. The next item on the agenda, after the inauguration, was a solo performance of a famous film song by one of the female students. There was tremendous applause from the audience when she finished and it woke up Dr Ramakrishnan. He realised that the next item on the agenda was his vote of thanks and conclusion speech. Unfortunately, he had not heard Dr Varughese correcting his previous mistake. He stood up and said, 'I thank all of you who came today to attend this inauguration. I am most grateful to Dr Samuel Jacob, the Vice Chancellor of Kerala University, who was gracious to accept our invitation and come here today to do the inauguration.'

The audience went wild with laughter, whistling and heckling. The principal looked totally confused as to why the audience was behaving boorishly!

The Swelling on the Neck

Rajan Abraham was a student in the college of dentistry that was attached to the Trivandrum Medical College, in Kerala, India. The two institutions were under Kerala University and they shared the same campus. It was convenient for the students of the dental college because they had to go to the surgical wards in the medical college hospital for their clinical posting to see patients with diseases of the head and neck.

Rajan loved his posting in the surgical wards. He had hoped to get admission to the medical college and become a cardiac surgeon but he didn't get through the entrance examination. He had to settle for a more modest ambition and become a dentist.

On his first day in the surgical wards, the associate professor in general surgery brought before Rajan and his fellow dental students, a patient who had goitre, a large orange sized swelling on the front of the neck. The students were asked to examine the patient and be ready with a diagnosis in about fifteen minutes. When the other students were busy examining the patient Rajan didn't bother. He took one look at the neck of the patient and the swelling which was clearly visible and decided that he knew the answer.

Unknown to his friends, Rajan had a private consultation with a consultant surgeon a few weeks ago about a similar swelling (of almost the same size and shape) he was harbouring in his scrotum. After examining his private parts carefully the surgeon had told him that it was a 'hydrocele', a collection of fluid in the scrotal sac and that could easily be removed surgically if he found it too uncomfortable. Rajan declined any surgical remedy because he was totally asymptomatic.

Armed with his secret knowledge about an orange sized swelling, Rajan was ready when the associate professor returned to the cubicle where he had left the students and the patient with the goitre. He asked his charges, 'Who can tell me the diagnosis?'

Rajan declared, before any of his colleagues could say a word, 'It is a hydrocele,' not knowing that the term hydrocele was specifically used for the scrotal condition only.

The associate professor and the other students had a whale of a time laughing.

The Industrious Student

The public health lectures for the fourth year medical students were usually delivered by the tutors or junior lecturers. They were so boring to the students that a good many of them (of the male species) would entertain themselves during this period talking among themselves or creating some mischief or other. If Prof Joseph Koshy, the head of the department, was doing the lecture there would be pin drop silence.

To deal with the unpleasant situation and avoid anarchy in her classroom, Dr Jayalaksmi, one of the tutors, allowed anyone who wanted to leave the hall to do so after their attendance was noted. The young ladies declined the offer but several of the young men, the chronic troublemakers, regularly left after making sure that their attendance was recorded; 80% attendance, in addition to pass marks in the examinations, was a compulsory requirement to clear any subject.

One day after the names were called out and attendance recorded, a bunch of students marched out as usual. They didn't realise that Prof Koshy was waiting outside to catch the culprits. The first one out through the doors was George Chacko. He was confronted by the professor. George was stunned and almost fainted. His friends behind him rapidly withdrew back into the lecture hall. Prof Koshy asked him, 'Are you boycotting the lecture?'

'No, sir, I was... I was going to the library,' George said, thinking this would be an acceptable explanation. He looked pale and white as a sheet of paper as if all the blood had drained away from his face.

'Oh! The library! Good. Good. Hey, you look very pale. I wonder if you have some intestinal parasites. It is very common in these parts you know. Certainly, you look very pale.' The public health professor relished speaking with his tongue in his cheek. He paused for a moment and then continued.

'I'll tell you what. Why don't you go to the library and read all about worms, round worms, hookworms, tapeworms, ringworms, the lot. When you have finish reading come to my office. I'll ask you some questions to test your knowledge as to what you have learned from the library.'

'Yes, sir,' the hapless George blurted out.

The Former Classmate

Subhash Bose was on summer vacation. The third year medical students had no scheduled activity that summer and he was at home to spend some time with his parents. One day he was out in the village with a bunch of his friends. They were at Kalathoor junction observing a protest meeting organised by the local branch of the Indian National Congress Party. There were several speakers, all denouncing the uncontrolled inflation and the inability of the ruling communist government to do anything about the rising cost of essential goods in the shops. It was a peaceful protest meeting. Subhash and the young men with him were not all that keen on political speeches, they were just watching the crowd and passing comments on the attendees, especially the young women. That was when a passing state transport bus stopped at the junction.

Subhash was standing a few yards away from the bus on the pavement meant for pedestrians. The bus had stopped for some passengers to alight and some others to hop on for the onward journey. That was when he noticed one of his former classmates, Alice Jacob, sitting at a window seat not far from where he was standing.

Alice had been his classmate three years ago before he got admission to the medical college. They were in the same batch of students reading chemistry. In fact, there were only twenty-two students in their batch, ten of whom were young ladies. During the three years they spent in the classroom together, Subhash had seldom spoken to Alice. It was a very conservative society where speaking to a young woman too often would be sufficient to spread rumours and tarnish her reputation.

Now that he was a medical student Subhash felt proud of himself and confident to talk to Alice, his former classmate. He knew that she would be pleased to see him too. He also wanted to show the friends with him that he could befriend ladies at will. Before the bus started moving again he rushed to Alice and said, 'Hey, Alice!'

Alice was a long-suffering motion sickness patient. That day she was feeling desperately nauseous and was waiting for the bus to stop somewhere to empty a mouthful of vomit. Unfortunately, she was not prepared or equipped with a plastic bag, and letting the contents of her mouth out when the bus was in full flight was not an option for fear for the people sitting in the seats around her. Now that the bus was stationary she leaned out of the window and got it all out on to the pavement, just as her old classmate was approaching her to renew their acquaintance. Subhash stepped back instinctively but it was not a pleasant spectacle to behold. His friends roared with laughter, seeing the would-be doctor embarrassed and… a bit wet.

The Winning Team

It was a winning team. Almost every trophy awarded for intercollegiate basketball competitions that year in Kerala was won by that team of eminent players. The nucleus of the team at St. Mathew's College, Changanacherrry, were five brilliant individuals, one of whom was my roommate in the men's hostel. No wonder I made it a point to go and watch numerous matches in different venues in various places.

When the team won the university championship I was there as well to witness that historic achievement at Kottayam CMS College grounds. The supporters who had accompanied the team were delirious with overwhelming joy. On our way back we decided that we would approach the college principal and ask him to declare the next day a holiday to honour our distinguished winning team; in those days an unscheduled holiday, for any reason, was most welcome.

Alas, the principal was away on leave. Worse still, Father Joseph Vettukattil, the vice principal, was in charge. He was an elderly gentleman with no interest in any kind of sporting activities whatsoever. Still, it was worth a try to approach him and find out his response to our request. We went to his office just as he was about to leave and told him the good news.

'Father, we won the match! We are the university basketball champions!'

'Oh, well done!' he said and followed up his answer with a question. 'How many goals did you score?'

Suppressing our urge to laugh, we politely reminded him, 'Father this was a game of basketball.'

'Oh! Sorry, I thought it was volleyball,' he said apologetically.

The Loving Boyfriend

Dr Thomas Chandy was a frustrated senior house officer. In spite of his experience and qualifications he was unable to go up the career ladder in orthopaedics. At that time the National Health Service (NHS) in England was desperately short of general practitioners (GPs) so he decided to apply for a training post to become a GP. At the interview he impressed the panel as a sincere and hardworking doctor with postgraduate qualifications in surgery who was keen to have a stab at a different speciality for career progression. He got selected but was to have further training in various other specialities in keeping with the GP training requirements.

His first posting was in gynaecology and obstetrics. There he had to spend some time in the labour room and attend a certain number of delivery cases. That was where Dr Chandy came across a young blonde woman, Claire, with her blonde boyfriend, Tom. He thought that Claire was exceptionally lucky to have such a loving boyfriend. There was kissing and cuddling and heavy petting during several hours in the labour room. When the contractions and subsequent cries of anguish were increasing in number, Tom was most supportive. He was holding her hands and encouraging her to push harder.

'Won't be long now, darling,' he kept saying to Claire.

After another few hours the ordeal of labour was about to end. With one last push the baby slowly emerged. The blonde boyfriend had one look at the just delivered brown coloured, Asian-looking baby and he let go of his girlfriend's hands saying, 'Sh**.'

As he quickly made his way towards the exit doors, Claire said loudly, 'Tom, I can explain.'

The blonde boyfriend left the labour room without saying a word to the nurses, doctors or his girlfriend.

What Shall I Call You?

The venue was the medical college auditorium, in Trivandrum, Kerala. The occasion was the fiftieth anniversary of the arts club, and the opportunity to perform in front of a distinguished array of invited guests, including the principal and professors of various departments, was considered a proud privilege. The senior students would normally get the coveted slots in the agenda and the juniors would have to wait for their chance the next year or the year after.

There are always exceptions to these unwritten rules. Sally George, a first year student, was the daughter of the home minister of Kerala State. She was also an excellent singer. She didn't have to ask for an opportunity to get on stage that day. The secretary of the arts club had approached her and asked, 'Would you like to sing your favourite song on the stage during the anniversary celebration of the arts club?'

Sally was a bit apprehensive because she was only a first year student and the response of the audience could be intimidating. She loved singing though and she found it impossible to refuse the offer of an opportunity to perform in front of an audience of eminent individuals.

'Yes, I would love to,' Sally agreed.

She selected a song from a famous Malayalam movie beginning 'ninne njaan entu vilikkum?' (What shall I call you?) It was a sweet, melodious song.

Sally was a beautiful young lady and she was dressed in a fabulous golden-yellow sari. On the stage in front of the microphone Sally was a pretty picture indeed. In her lovely voice she slowly sang the first line, 'What shall I call you?' She was about to begin the second line when a third year student, who had never met her before, stood up in the audience and shouted in a loud voice, 'Call me Mathew now. After the marriage you have to call me "Achaya",' (a respectful way some Christian wives address their husbands in Kerala).

The audience went wild with laughter and catcalls.

The Reconciliation

Philip was not on good terms with his neighbour Alice. It all started after their children had a fight in the school playground. The parents got involved and even after the children made up their differences and became friends again the adults couldn't bring themselves to talk to one another. Alice was a widow and she was a very reserved type of woman. Philip's wife Christine had given strict instructions to her husband (who she knew was a 'softie') not to talk to Alice, who was only a few years older than him, anymore. For over a year the neighbours were not on speaking terms, even though on Sundays they regularly attended the same parish of the Syrian Orthodox Church in Cochin, Kerala, India.

One Sunday the sermon was about the 'Lord's Prayer'. The vicar reminded his flock that Jesus taught his disciples about the need to forgive one another. Every time they said the Lord's Prayer they were saying 'Forgive our trespasses as we forgive those who trespass against us'. Those who were asking for God's forgiveness in that prayer were also claiming that they regularly forgave others who had wronged them.

Philp wondered if the vicar was looking at him throughout the sermon and was calling on him to forgive his neighbour. He decided to overrule his wife's edict and reconcile with Alice.

He was walking home alone because his wife had stayed behind to attend a meeting of the 'ladies home group' in the church. After a while he saw Alice who had walked ahead of him. Alice was desperate to pee and she had sat down behind a bush in her compound not far from the walkway because she didn't think she would make it to the toilet in her house in time. Philip saw Alice sitting there but didn't realise that she was answering a call of nature. Determined that he was going to make up with the woman, he asked her, 'Cheduthi (respected sister), how are you doing?'

The woman, who had seen no one around before she sat down, pulled up her knickers and stood up instantly, unleashing a torrent of abuse at Philip calling him a dirty Peeping Tom.

Acknowledgement

I am grateful to David Morrison of PublishNation who kindly undertook to publish and promote this work. I thank Almighty God for all the blessings I have had in my life, including my interest in creative wring.

Printed in Great Britain
by Amazon

41565113R00056